PARADISE LOST

KYLE SWIGART

Olympus Story House

Contents

Disclaimer

The contents of this work, including, but not limited to, the accuracy of events, people, and places depicted; opinions expressed; permission to use previously published materials included; and any advice given or actions advocated are solely the responsibility of the author, who assumes all liability for said work and indemnifies the publisher against any claims stemming from publication of the work.

Dedication

This book is dedicated to the people who feel they have no purpose in
life or feel there's nobody who cared to find out
what their purpose may be.

Paradise Lost

I have no master's or PhD, I didn't go to Harvard or any other IVY league school; my words come from my heart and own life experiences and adversities that I have gone through in my life. Adversities help define and mold your life for the good and bad. They help you learn how to cope with stress, rebound from difficult times in your life. For the majority of the world's population, struggle is an everyday part of life; some struggle to hold a job, some struggle to stay away from drugs even though they know where they will end up. Others struggle with trying to keep faithful to their better half. Some struggle to put enough food on plates to feed their family. We all struggle in some way or form, we all deal with trauma in different ways some more positive than others—it all depends on our own personal perspective. We are all individuals in our own right; what one person may regard as a positive release from our daily struggles might seem as a negative to another. Some use alcohol and drugs as a way to relieve themselves of the daily struggles, while others use drugs and alcohol for the simple reason: they like how it feels. Others are just plain addicted to it and let the drugs and alcohol take over their lives. For the majority of people who are addicted, it's a disease that has been with them since the day they were born. It's just part of one's DNA. The problem is they may never be aware of this disease until it was too late, and the drugs got ahold of them. Being aware that you may have an addictive personality should help you realize that all it's going to take is once, and the rest of your life may be spent being in a drug-induced coma.

Our ability to deal with struggle and strife comes from a large part of our environment and past experiences. I don't claim to be a psychologist, nor do I have a PhD. I can only speak from my past environment and experiences, which has helped me deal with the everyday struggles of life. My story is about my struggle in Hawaii, where most people think of it as paradise on a postcard, with an ice-cold beer on a white sand beach with the palm trees blowing in the wind with beautiful woman dancing hula and blowing kisses. That postcard reality may be for some who could buy their plastic relationships and ocean view houses, but that wasn't my reality. Growing up was a real struggle mentally and physically. Battling racial discrimination and a broken home on a daily basis tested my resolve. When I look back on it, I wouldn't change anything. Maybe I would have caught the football more times then I dropped it, but that's about it. I look back at my life now and realize all that struggle and strife has made me stronger, self-resilient. At the same time, I also wouldn't want my children to face the same discrimination and struggles I faced. My life's struggles shaped me but don't define who I am and my ability to achieve my goals. Though my losses and defeats, I'm able to take on any obstacle that comes my way and able to take a loss and keep a smile on my face. If you never faced struggle or strife as an adolescent, how will you be able to face it as an adult? It was a question I struggled with for many years of my life. Why me? How would my life turn out differently if I had 10 percent of what the other kids got. What if I had never faced any racial discrimination, that made me question my self-worth for many years? It took me a long time and self-evaluation to realize that without those life experiences caused by the environment that I was in I wouldn't be the person that I am today. I'm not writing this book to say that my life was any harder than anybody else's, just trying to make people aware that we all face some sort of struggle and strife, no matter where we live and what color we may be. It's the level of struggle or even the perception that people may have that those struggles were that allows one to move on with our losses. Prejudice is not based on color, but on the ignorance of the human race. I had to fight to get respect and this I hold to my heart because when you lose everything all you got is your pride, and that's something nobody can take from you.

For me this book is about coming to grips with the past. As I got older, I started to realize I was having a hard time trying to remember my past childhood and adolesence, trying to put bits and pieces together. It's our natural instinct to shove bad experiences into a place in our memory where we never want to think about them again. As I got older,

I began to realize I needed to deal with these emotions, or let it eat me up inside. Writing has become my way of expressing my hardships and confronting the pain that I have buried for the majority of my life in a healthy way. Also, by sharing my life experiences, it may help someone facing the same type of feelings. It was my self-defense in coping with it, but that anger only eats at you slowly until you explode on your family and friends who were only trying to help. I spent many years avoiding my past, getting angry at my sister for anything she would say or do. She never deserved any of the anger or frustration I showed, but when your life is in a constant state of confusion you don't know any better. I spent so much time trying to make a life for myself, I didn't pay enough attention to my only brother and the importance of letting your loved ones know you love them. Friends would talk about their past childhood experiences and adolescence, and I would have nothing to say, making me feel jealous and angry for missing out on the good times. Adolescence seemed a blur, barely able to remember bits and pieces of it. It's the body's way of dealing with trauma. I still question what's more painful, physical or mental abuse, while I only dealt with mental abuse from my father, they both leave a lasting effect. But as I grew older, and seeing the pain and suffering I caused, I realized I needed let go of what happened to my adolescence. There were good and times and bad times. I can never forget the how I would always end up with a Mountain Dew at the end of a long hard day of yardwork with my father who instilled in my hard-working attitude. Now I remember where my childhood went to helping my father in his yard cleaning service. I'm being cynical, it wasn't that bad; I was still able to play soccer and surf on the weekends. My best friend growing up was JapaneseHawaiian boy named Mokie. He was my neighbor, only living two houses down. I was the only white boy in the neighborhood. I heard Haole many times, sometimes used derogatory against me or in a conversation I was involved in at a young age. The word Haole was something you grow accustomed to over the years. When I was young, I got mad and frustrated as you feel like you were never welcome. The stigmatism stays with no matter old you get. The anger goes away, but the hurt never leaves. You realize it's the culture you live in and ignorance that people have that can't be changed. It's taught from generation to generation. While the word "Haole" means foreigner, its used as a derogatory term toward a Caucasian. There were many times that we get in a fight with my best friend and he call me F## haole "go back where you came from" and we wouldn't talk for weeks. Ignoring each other as if we never saw each other, even though we lived

3

only two houses apart. But as most child buddies do, we would forget about our arguments. If we weren't spending our time fighting chickens with neighborhood rivals, it was playing football or basketball with the rest of the neighborhood kids. We played football anyplace there was room, sometimes on the asphalt street or the nearest grass we could find. Though sometimes these football games got a little intense and were the cause of many fights. Two hand touch turned into tackle on many occasions.

He could remember going to the beach together. My favorite beach was on the west side named Pakala's. It was known for its chocolate brown water and perfect peeling lefts which you could ride for days. Pakala's had its dangers inside and outside of the water. If the bulls lingering around the trail on the way in didn't scare you, then you would be taking your chances with the fierce and friary locals in the water. Although before we ever went to Pakala's, my dad would always check if we were wearing red. I always thought it was pretty ridiculous on his part when I was kid, until saw bullfighting on TV and realized there was a reason my dad would always tell us this. Me and the rest of my family would walk down the trail with my dad in the front, when all a sudden his father with a deep and riveting voice yelled, "Stop where you and don't move, there's a bull on the trail." Me being the wise mouth kid I was, answered back with "Yeah, sure there is, right next to the giraffe." I walked a little closer to my father as my eyes zeroed in with complete concentration on this enormous beast, saliva dripping from his mouth and a mouth full of grass as he just stared at us with his sharp horns. He looked as big as a tractor with little or no fat to be seen by the naked eye. He stood on the trail as if he knew he was the boss and nobody was going to tell him to move, occasionally looking up at us with his grinding teeth and dripping mouth to make sure we weren't going to try anything foolish. I asked my father, "So what are we going to do now?" (Me wasn't the most patient child.) He said, "We're going to wait until he decides that it's time for him to move, and don't make any sudden movements." Thirty minutes later the massive beast relinquished his position on the trail and moved on to terrorize another day. The trail was engulfed with qiney grass that had scissor like leaves that would leave paper like cuts on your hand if you tried to touch it. The giney grass on both sides was so high that you couldn't see what's lying behind the giney grass. As we walked down the trail, I asked my father if the bull was always here when he came. He said, "Yes, but don't worry because he won't bother you unless you bother him." A good lesson learned in life.

4

Getting past the bull was only the first step in this journey of life. We got to the beach, and to my surprise, this wasn't your typical picturesque Hawaiian beach. The water was a brown color, barely clear enough to see your hand in the water. The only thing was missing was a sign saying, "Enter at your own risk, if you dare." Compared to what I was used to on the east side, where there was turquoise blue water with beautiful white sand. It felt very alien to me. Even the smell of the beach was different. Usually the smell of sunscreen overwhelms most beaches, but Pakalas was different; it had a very distinct smell of seaweed and salt in the air.

As you walked along the beach it very ire feeling, as you could see the seaweed along the shoreline with lobster's shells and the occasional dead baby hammerhead shark, that was caught the night before by the local fishermen. As we walked down the beach to find our spot to put our belongings, I could see the perfect peeling lefts with only wonder. Waves this perfect are only in magazines, not on the island of Kauai I thought. I asked my father, "Why are there some many lobster shells on the beach?" and he said, "Because the lobsters shed their shells." I also asked about the dead shark, and he said, "It was probably caught by a fishermen and didn't want throw it back in the water." What a waste of animal, I thought. Seeing the dead shark gave me second thoughts about going into water you can barely see your hand in, even if the dead shark was only two feet. We reached our spot on the beach and sat down. We helped set up the chairs so my mom could relax, even though I knew she would be worrying about me every second I was out there being tested. That's how she was, no matter what, she always worried about her children. I can remember she made me sign a paper saying that I will not ride any type of motorcycle until I was eighteen years old. I did reluctantly, even though I was dying to ride one and eventually go on one after turning 18 years old. At the time I didn't understand the deep love parents have for their children, but now that I have children I see where the worry and love comes from.

We sat and just watched the waves for a good fifteen minutes, as this was something my dad could do for long time. He could spend waiting hours on the beach just waiting for the right tide or the winds to turn offshore and turn a mediocre wave into made only in magazines. Being an inpatient adolescent, it drove me nuts that he could just sit there and watch these perfect peeling waves come in and not want to be riding them instantly, and the funny thing is he can still there just watching the waves for hours as the waves put him into a trance, but that's the beauty of getting older, you learn to appreciate the smaller things in life. I was getting impatient with just watching so I said, "I'm going out, Dad, I can't take this anymore." I couldn't help it, the waves were like something from a movie, wave after wave. He said, "You need to watch the waves and study them before you go out." "Study what?" was my response, like any adolescent thinking they know everything. "You need to look at the current and where the waves are breaking." I lasted five more minutes and I was paddling out with my dad close behind. I'm pretty sure my mom was telling him to stay close behind me. I was like the Energizer bunny, just filled with energy. My heart was pumping hard and fast, I could hear my own heartbeat. It didn't take long before we were out investigating the line up. It was filled with large men with huge longboards and the funny thing is, the line up hasn't changed much. Me and my father must have been only two light-skinned people in the water or "Hoale," depending on who you ask. They all looked very intimidating, with large wide shoulders and shaved heads, but the waves were too good to just watch, so I started paddling toward the crowd, and soon I was getting deep fierce looks; they didn't have to say a word to express how they felt. I was a new face, invading their territory. As I paddled closer one of the large gentlemen said, "You better watch yourself, kid." I countered with, "I will do my best," and kept on paddling. This was another test, I needed to show respect but show them that I want to be here just as much as them. Which is key; in Hawaii and in the water, respect isn't given by how much money you make or who your parents where, respect is earned, never granted to you by your place in society. So that's what I did, I caught waves that went unridden no matter how big or small. I took my hard knocks but kept on catching waves. Catching that perfect right for first time, feeling that offshore winds in my face as I flew down section after section with reckless abandonment was a feeling of ecstasy. It's that feeling I get every time I surf Pakala's. A feeling that nobody can take away, even when you're having the worst day of your life, and nothing seems to be going your way, all you need is one of those perfect rights and all is forgotten, at least the time that is spent in that murky brown water. The first couple times out at Pakala's was like being on a tight rope, never really knowing if you're going in with a beautiful wave or a black eye. The hard stares turned to smiles the more time I spent at Pakala's, enjoying paradise. The ocean demands respect and so do the people who enjoy its beauty. It's all about paying your dues.

Chapter One

My childhood really got flipped upside down and inside out without any explanation on what seemed to be a typical day in paradise, clear blue skies and trade winds blowing strong in my face as I sat in the passenger seat as my dad had just picked me up from the airport as I had just arrived from spending a month on Guam where I was conceived and born. The trip was an eye opener for him. His godfather was a very unique and very kind individual that I enjoyed spending time with. He had a special aura about him that made him shine with a happiness that made me want to emulate him in many ways. He was a water lover just like me. Every new adventure featured new experiences. Whether it was seeing the huge coconut crabs that could take your finger off without a struggle or the trips through the mangroves that reminded of a scene from Star Wars, where Luke meets Yoda for the first time. These coconut crabs looked like hermit crabs on steroids. Although he told me that they were delicious, I was not about to take my uncle up on it. I was content with watching them from afar. They were slow but had claws the size of my arm, it seemed like a science experiment gone wrong. The trip through the mangroves of Palau was a blast from the past with a dense canopy of trees that kept the sunlight out and murky brown water below. It was my godfather, myself, and the guide in a wooden canoe that was barely big enough for three. As that went through the mangroves, the guide often checked his crab traps looking for Samoan crabs, which are not as giant as the coconut crab, but just as menacing in their own right. It was a trip to remember. Coming off the plane, he was in high spirits, but that was soon to change. As I sat there with a smile, I thought about all the awesome adventures I had just been with my Godfather James and was hoping the summer would be just as fun, then with the sternest voice I had ever heard my father speak with he said, "Son, I need to let to know something. Your mother and I have separated and she moved out to house down the road." I just sat there like I just got hit with wrecking ball, all the life in me just ripped out. I was ill prepared for those words. My eyes looked empty with despair as tears ran down my face. My body became numb with sadness. I couldn't talk or even look at my father as my anger began to get the better of me. That moment shattered my world, flipped it upside down, and what came next was a lot of time trying to find myself and where I belonged. Life as a teenager was already difficult but feel so alone and isolated made it tough. From that moment on, life would never be same.

My father was not the most communicative person, so all questions that were starting to form in my head would have to be figured out by myself. Why is this happening to me? What could I have done to prevent it? How can this be fixed? The typical questions that every child seems to have when everything they knew and cherished gets flipped and there's no explanation. All these questions were answered as time went on and I matured, but it was difficult having to find out these answers on my own was a journey to finding owns personal strength. I spend a long time blaming myself for the circumstances and being angry at myself and everybody around you even though they had no control over the circumstances or the actions of others. But realizing it's not your fault is paramount in walking out of that dark world of pain and despair! While pain is an inedible part of life, it doesn't have to surround your every decision.

I was thirteen years old when I was told the shocking news by my father. I was not prepared at all for the next period of my life, but there's no preparing for years of hurt loneliness. Anger can be good and bad; it's how you use it. I used it very negatively, trying to hurt everybody around either verbally or through my actions. I started hanging around people going with no direction like me, and it started with small things at school like bad grades and poor attendance in school, to breaking and entering of automobiles before made a few changes in my life.

While I wasn't the only white boy in the whole school, I was one of the poorest though. I didn't fit in with the rest of the white boys, I wasn't from the north shore, which is where of most of the white kids lived, I never had a car to drive in high school and walked home daily. It's amazing how money can get you all the friends in the world, while they may or may not be your real friends at that age, you really don't know what true friendship means. I wasn't Hawaiian, Japanese or Filipino. Who could I relate to? Who was I, a child with no self-esteem or guidance. I wasn't comfortable in my own skin and felt very alone. But I was pretty lucky, though, my bestfriend and neighbor throughout my childhood and adolescence was Hawaiian and Japanese. His family treated me like one their own and taught me the ways of the Hawaiian culture. They would go camping trips to the beach on the weekends, and I would always be invited. It's there I learned about fishing and diving and respecting the ocean. We would go diving at night with a three-prong spear and spear what we would eat for dinner that night. I learned what fish was good to eat and what wasn't, but also to take only take what you're going to eat. Always leaving the reef how you found it was so that the future generation may have the same opportunity I had was something Mokie's dad taught me. Mokie's dad took us out in the beginning to guide us and keep an eye on us, but the more we went, the more he became confident in us going without him. While Mokie's ohana treated me like their own, that wasn't always the case outside of the Miyashiro ohana, as no matter how much I wanted to be an equal, it seemed I was always looked as inferior to the other students because of my skin color. I was always having to defend himself, in school, in the neighborhood, it seemed the whole world was against me at times. Always looking from the outside in. I needed to be strong if he was going to survive in this environment. It's the start of ninth grade and my family situation is only getting worse. My mother's drinking worsening, and the fire within him is burning hotter. He remembers seeing his mother drunk on a nightly basis, some nights worse than others. On nights, my mother would become so intoxicated that she was fall on her face and dream the pain away. The love I had for my mother was turning into hate, and there was no end in sight. What could I do, I tried everything I could think of to make it stop. My sister and I searched the house up and down for the wine bottles and dump them out as fast as he could find them, but to no avail there seemed to be some secret stash that only my mother knew of and the race to get intoxicated began. The defeating and helpless feeling trying to help someone you love from seeing them fall on their face night after night and eventually knock out on the floor was one of the most painful memories I live with today. Without guidance and direction in his life, he began finding ways to get attention in the wrong ways. Like him, his circle of friends had come from dysfunctional families. It started with innocent pranks, like egging houses at night. We would pull up to somebody from high school who wasn't particular liked by the Three Amigos and throw as many eggs at the target as they could find in the refrigerator. The leader of the Three Amigos went by the name of Keoni, would was the organizer of the three. Even in school they were finding ways to get into trouble. The librarians were getting to know the group well. We would break stink bombs in the library that caused the whole library to evacuate. One person would occupy the librarian, while his partner would find a well-populated spot in the library to break the tiny capsule that contained the foul odor. It was the funniest thing watching people run out of the library because of our stink bombs. As time went on and we didn't get caught, the more daring we got. But the fun in the library had to an end as the librarians caught on to the fun. Punishment was no fun as we spent hours helping the librarians stack everything by alphabetical order, but it helped me. realize that was one job that I was not going to do in the future. So stink bombs in the library ended, to the relief of the librarians, but it wasn't the end of things.

It seems that high school is a time of finding yourself and having fun doing it. It's hard to find yourself when you don't relate to the majority, and you feel like an outcast, and it feels like a battle that no matter what you can't win. But yet you endure and strive to succeed in what everybody around considers paradise. I really understand now how important it is to have strong role models in your life, or you could spend your whole life trying to find who you are.

Now it was time to become more daring. Ripping off emblems of luxury cars with the fancy rims and shiny paint jobs, which I seemed to admire, was the new fad. My total lack of respect toward anybody or their personal property was an easy way to defy everything that my father had tried to install in him. I wanted my father to hurt the way I hurt inside. It didn't matter where the high priced fancy emblems were, it was the Three Amigos new fancy. Yet I still wasn't satisfied. I couldn't seem to make my dad hurt the way I felt on the inside. There were times when I felt like a ghost in his father's eyes no matter how hard he tried to get attention with his antics. Not spoken to for months because I decided one morning I didn't feel like waking up before the crack of dawn and joining my father on a surf trip to Pakala's. As you grow up, you notice how these small things in a child's life can leave a lasting memory whether it's good or bad. Like any fad the emblems were becoming boring, and there needed to be a replacement. Stealing from convenient stores became the next best thing. Weekend raids on these newfound resources became a regular. Each time trying time to up on another to see who could get away with the most possessions without getting caught. Occasionally the local gas station would have sodas stocked on the outside, leaving a easy target for the Three Amigos. One would keep the gas attendant busy while the others would be stacking the car with soda boxes as fast as possible. There were plenty of close calls, but know hard time for the three amigos. By his sophomore year things at home only deteriorated, the feeling of abandonment and despair were only getting stronger. My parents only spoke because they had to, and I seemed to be in the crossfire of a raging war of who's paying who and how much. Letting their anger toward each other get the better of each other and forgetting about the pain and suffering they were causing the rest of the family. Anger has a great way of letting you forget about the people around you that you hurt to try and make yourself happy, even though it's a fake happiness.

There was a glimmer of hope for me. My sister and my extended family constantly tried to reach out to help this directionless child. I didn't listen, I was in his own world, unable to see through the dark cloud. My anger and frustration consumed his ability to care about the people around me who were trying to show their love. As one matures in life, it's easy to see where one's vision can get clouded and bury.

What could be next for the Three Amigos? Like any other teenagers sooner or later, the convenient stores would lose their allure, and compliancy would draw them into something else. Breaking into automobiles, looking for that cold hard cash were next. While cash was the primary objective, personal valuables also worked. Though sooner or later the luck would have to run out and it had. While searching a rental car at a local hotel, a female who was working for the approached the car being searched, and questioned me and my partners in crime about their activities. Acting quickly, I persuaded the female in believing that the cars was their relative's and were only retrieving was their's. She told them that she was going to check on it and would return. Once she left they ran as fast as they could to the second amigo's house. They thought they had gotten away with another great heist. To their surprise, as they were hanging outside the house, the enraged female was pulling into the neighbor's garage and noticed the two juveniles standing in the garage. She immediately came over and ordered to speak to our parents. She explained to our parents what had happened and left the punishment in their hands. On the ride home, very few words were spoken between me and my dad, but the disappointment in his father's face was obvious. It didn't faze me. All I could think about was getting revenge for getting him in trouble. Instead of facing his responsibilities and realizing the road

11

he was taking was going nowhere, I began planning his revenge. Like any other disillusioned juvenile with no appreciable adult guidance, all the pain I caused upon others went unnoticed. The following weekend the Three Amigos went looking for revenge and I found it in the keying of the woman's vehicle. I got his revenge, but I was in for the shock of his young life as I was woken up to the sound of a police officer knocking on his doorstep.

I looked outside in fear, as he knew what the police officer was there for. There was no place for me to run this time. He faced his responsibilities for the first time and opened the door. His younger sister was the only one home at the time. The officer questioned me about the night before, and I confessed of all my wrongdoings. I knew the time was going to come and the day had finally come. I was brought to the police station and booked. As I was driven to the police station, the police officer talked to me about my activity and what I was doing was only going to lead him into a life of darkness and sorrow. I wish I could have remembered the officer's name because he helped me be a better person. Something was finally getting through my jaded mind. As I listened, things were sinking in. I never imagined my actions would lead me to be taken away from my own home in a police car and taken to get fingerprinted as the neighbors watched. I knew sooner rather than later my activities would lead me to this day. Being arrested was a turning point in my life. I knew he had to find some positive way to direct his anger and pain. I found it in football. With each hit I delivered, he felt the pain and anger being released toward somebody else: my parents. My date with the judge came at the beginning of the season. I walked into the judge quarters pondering what would become of my past actions. Was I to do time in juvenile hall? Not likely for a first offense. But there are a million things running through your mind when faced with the fact that you must accept responsibilities for your actions when you never have. The judge talked to me and asked me what was I doing that would keep me from participating in delinquent behavior. I told the judge I was playing football now and I found a way of dealing with the anger through football. Apparently, the judge saw the sincerity in his eyes and let me go with a verbal warning.

This was a great lesson for me. The delinquent activities had finished, as football was taking the majority of his time. I wasn't the biggest nor the fastest, but I had the fire within. No matter how big or small I was going to be hit or hit somebody. Being one of the only white guys and of the smallest made for a huge challenge to prove that he could play.

Before I ever put a step on that grassy field, there were pre-conceived notions because of his race that I couldn't run as fast, catch as well, or hit like the rest of the players. It seemed the bigger players were always looking for me, but I was quick on my feet and never let them get a clear shot on me. But when I did get hard, I would get right back up and complement them on the hit, letting them know that I was ready to battle again. The classic case of the underdog showing that I was not going to back down no matter what came my way. They tried and tried to break my spirit, but I kept on getting up no matter how much pain I was in. There were numerous times that I would sit down in the locker room after practice and think to myself, Is this worth it? I needed to prove to myself and the rest of my teammates that I was here to stay. To quit now would mean defeat, showing that all those people who doubted me were right. As the season went on, I earned the respect of the players. I showed my teammates that I was just as strong as them and the color of my skin was not a sign of weakness. In Hawaii respect isn't given, it's earned, through some hard knocks and the understanding of one's culture. Throughout the season his relationship with my father became more distant as time went on. I can remember going to games and looking up in the stands hoping to see at least one of my parents at the game. I can always remember my mom saying how everyone looked so big compared to me, and how she that I was so brave playing against them. I'm sure she was always nervous about me getting hurt, as she always knew I was a rebel. My mother made me sign a paper saying I wouldn't get a motorcycle until I was eighteen years old. My father never took much interest in my life unless it dealt with surfing, which made me dislike surfing for years to come. While surfing would become a savior in my life later on, for now it left a bitter taste every time I looked at the ocean, even though it was my playground during his early years. I can remember being ignored for months by my father for not wanting to go surfing with him one early weekend morning. Memories like this last a lifetime. To be treated as a ghost by your own father was a stepping stone into realizing that I was basically on my own, and only person I could count on was myself. My mother tried to give as much love as she could, but the anger that was boiling inside every time he came home to a mother slurring and barely being able to stand up on her own two feet because of her intoxication was taking pushing the love away. There were times when me and my sister would search the whole house trying to find all the hidden wine. I would destroy as much as he could find, only to find his mother in the same intoxicated state as the night

13

before. I would spend some nights crying myself to sleep to take away the pain. How can somebody who is supposed to love you with all their heart put you though that type of pain and anguish? Maybe they don't understand what they are doing to their child and how it's going to affect them for the rest of their life. I understand now that she wasn't trying to punish me or my sister or brother; she had no control over her disease. It was her way of dealing with the her life struggles and the environment that she was presently in. But though all the pain and anguish I have been able to find a shining light that has helped look at the situation and find the positive out of the whole situation. That saying, "What doesn't kill you can only make you stronger," has been the story of my life. I was able to survive in a world where all the odds were against me, and come out with scratches and bruises, that will heal in time keeping my head high and proud. I believe now, I was put through the struggles to make me a stronger and better person. Having been through hardship allows to have empathy and compassion for others. I know that in this world anything is possible if you want, but you need to be able to work for it because if it comes too easy you won't appreciate it as much. I graduated high school, didn't have the best grades, but my expectations for myself at that age weren't very high. I had no intentions or want of going to college at the time and was intent with trying to work things out and figure out who I was. My self-worth or self-esteem coming out of high school was pretty low. I had no leadership or guidance throughout my high school years. Even my guidance counselor in high school wrote me off. My grades weren't anything to be looked at or to be admired. I felt very alone and isolated at that point in my life.

Something deep inside me didn't let fail or give up on myself. I had a drive to succeed in life, some way, somehow, I was going to make something out of my life. I enrolled in the junior college and joined the National Guard after a few semesters at the community college, realizing to graduate from school I was going to have to pay for it myself. I was off to boot camp at Fort Benning, Georgia, to become an 11B infantry man in the Hawaii National Guard. A huge culture shock coming from an island surrounded by a body of water. Being thrown into what the drill sergeant called a "cattle truck" was my first of many life-changing experiences in the military. It's called a cattle truck due to the fact that the trailer your maneuvered into resembles the same type of trailer live cattle are rounded up and sent to the slaughter house in. A scary thought for a nineteen-year-old being away from home for the first time in his life. I made it through basic training and the infantry school. I decided

14

that I wanted to become a firefighter and enrolled in classes to become one. I eventually got into the State of Hawaii Airport Fire Department, which help me become the family man I am today. I have been truly blessed in my life by many friends and family who have guided me throughout my path in life and help me become the person I am today.